Mumin Mindset

The Mindset of a Muslim Man destined for Greatness.

Written by s.hukr

Mumin Mindset

السلام عليكم

I hope you find peace, wisdom, and love through these words.

I hope this book inspires you to love yourself, educate yourself and become a better Muslim.

May Allah guide you toward that which is best while making your Dunya and your Deen easy for you.

If there is a word that you do not understand, simply search the definition of the word on

Google.com

fajrnoor.com

Mumin Mindset

The men who chase wisdom,
wealth, power, love, piety, respect
and justice for the sake of Allah.

They are the real men you want
in your life. The rest are just
time wasters.

s.hukr

Mumin Mindset

You know what's dangerous?

Young Muslim men who have been given Amanah by Allah.

Men with hearts of pure gold, minds of solid steel and souls made from an abundant noor.

Men who will never show you their true power but only exercise God's will.

Beware of those men.
They exist.

s.hukr

Mumin Mindset

I think the most beneficial skill
that I have learned is the art
of self-learning.

The ability to learn without
the assistance of another human,
a teacher or an institution.

A skill that will empower you and
make you less reliant upon people
and more reliant upon Allah.

s.hukr

Mumin Mindset

You can't change and grow if you
think you know everything.
That's ego talking.

Silence your ego and listen to
your soul. It will naturally pull
you closer towards your
divine purpose.

s.hukr

Mumin Mindset

If you are looking for a wife,
make sure she has an abaya
or jilbab collection.

That's an easy green flag.

s.hukr

Mumin Mindset

Think of a human as a very intelligent and sophisticated computer. The hardware is your physical body. The mind is your operating system, and the heart is your power source.

If you have the best hardware, but the operating system has a virus. You will be self-sabotaging yourself. If you have the best mindset, but you lack will power, you will be afraid and insecure.

To ensure best performance from yourself, you must take care of your 3 most valuable assets.

Heart = Ethics & Morality
Mind = Knowledge & Awareness
Body = Exercise & Diet

s.hukr

Mumin Mindset

Money, status, and beauty.

You must never let these
seduce your soul.

Beware of people who
are slaves of their desires.

They are the sheep.
You must remain the lion.

s.hukr

Mumin Mindset

Make so much money but don't tell a soul.
Win so many hearts but don't tell a soul.
You don't need to tell people anything.

Silence is also an answer because your actions will speak louder than words ever could.

s.hukr

Mumin Mindset

Body of a warrior.
Mind of a stoic.
Heart of a Mumin.

That's the goal.

s.hukr

Mumin Mindset

Some people have families by the age of 25, working a job they hate and coming home to a house full of problems they want to run from.

Others will build empires, dynasties, and armies by the age of 25. They will inspire millions, move millions, and serve Allah to the best of their ability.

What will you do?

Waste your time on Tiktok?

s.hukr

Mumin Mindset

Riba is a war with Allah.
Don't even think about it.
Because you will never win.

s.hukr

Mumin Mindset

Men need to understand that when a
woman is stressed, she wants to talk,
and all you need to do is listen,
not to offer solutions.

s.hukr

Mumin Mindset

Men who are attracting a lot of women are men who are dominating their life purpose. They don't care about attracting women, they care about their purpose and passions in life.

s.hukr

Mumin Mindset

A woman is the best indicator of
how good a man is and vice versa.

So if you want to know a man's character,
ask a woman in his vicinity. She'll tell you
everything you need to know.

s.hukr

Mumin Mindset

Some are slaves of love.
Some are slaves of money.
Some are slaves of fear.
Some are slaves of ego.
Some are slaves of desire.

But I rather be a slave of Allah.

s.hukr

Mumin Mindset

Respect should never be forced or given for free. It must always be earned.

It must be in correlation with
the message of Islam.

s.hukr

Mumin Mindset

Be a man who has no desire to
be seen by the creation.

Who earns his Rizq through his worship.
Who is hard to reach and out of sight.

s.hukr

Mumin Mindset

Private conversations are sacred trusts.

The more trustworthy you become the more the Amanah will follow you.

s.hukr

Mumin Mindset

People want things quick and easy.
Nobody wants to be patient and hardworking.

You need patience for many years.
You need hard working for many years.

Things become quick and easy after you develop a strong level of patience and discipline.

s.hukr

Mumin Mindset

While you're spending 50k on her mahr,
there are people who have nothing.

While you're thinking of buying a luxury watch,
car or house, there are people who don't have
enough to survive tomorrow.

I'm not saying don't enjoy life,
I'm saying have a heart.

s.hukr

Mumin Mindset

Even if I was a millionaire, I would never give some outrage sum of money to my wife as a gift. I would give what is reasonable, what she is capable of handling without it effecting her Deen.

For Allah has made me the caretaker, the one in authority. If she refuses, it is her loss.

s.hukr

Mumin Mindset

Work so damn hard that one day
you don't have to introduce yourself.

s.hukr

Mumin Mindset

A true Muslim pursues a life of excellence, not perfection.

If you want true success, you must be hungry for excellence.

s.hukr

Mumin Mindset

A man's life is constant work.

We are always working towards something. It ranges from health, money, mindset, family, deen and community.

The more we work, the better life becomes for us and the people around us. There is nothing wrong with working if there is divine purpose. I speak for most men when I say we don't need vacations or holidays. We don't need a second wife or a man cave.

We just want to come home to a loving wife who becomes our peace and quiet. Our place of joy and happiness. The reason most men escape to a man cave or another relationship. It is because it stops becoming home.

s.hukr

Mumin Mindset

Reputation speaks volumes.

People don't need to know your family life, your private life, your likes, dislikes or your opinions. They just need to know if they can trust you. Whether or not you're a man of strong foundations or not.

If you're a man, I highly suggest you start building your reputation. Be genuine, be humble, be generous, be patient, be knowledgeable, be known for
all good qualities.

s.hukr

Mumin Mindset

Did the Prophet ever beat his children?

No. So why do I hear stories of parents beating their children?

Discipline doesn't require physical abuse. It requires love, repetition, and consistency.

Let that sink it.

s.hukr

Mumin Mindset

Gossip. I hate it.

I don't understand how someone can assume or suspect something bad about someone else without any verified evidence and then spread it. Doing haram in private is one thing.

But doing haram, making it public and hurting someone else's reputation is something else. That is the complete opposite of what Islam teaches us.

You should be ashamed of yourself if you allow this to happen in your presence.

s.hukr

Mumin Mindset

I've learned to just forgive, forget and move on with my life. I don't have time to start drama with people anymore.

I don't want to prove a point, to show people how I feel. I have surpassed all that nonsense.

I choose mercy, love and growth.
But I forget, not everyone is like me.

s.hukr

Mumin Mindset

Some people will always be a test for me.

But they best believe I will do my absolute best to pass the test. I will not allow people to destroy the good that I have built, and neither should you.

s.hukr

Mumin Mindset

I'm harsh with family but never without merit. It is sour love that turns sweet with time. You must hold your ground if you want to be a good leader. Women respect strong men who are firm on their values.

s.hukr

Mumin Mindset

Focused, disciplined and successful people don't have time to waste on people who are weak. They will abstain themselves from people and places that do not provide value.

They don't believe they are better than you. They simply do not like the idea of devaluing their time and the time of others.

By living this way, we have a better life. No chaos, no drama, no stress and no loss of time or money. No loss of good deeds.

We can invest into other areas of life which may become more fruitful for society. Instead of going to a wedding with music or having a gathering where gossip is normal.

Even right now, I'm spending my time writing this to educate and inspire you. I want to leave a positive legacy and use my time to promote a better mindset that will help you and everyone around you.

s.hukr

Mumin Mindset

As a man, you need to be extremely aware.

You need to be aware of what's happening at home, in the streets and in the world. You have a responsibility upon yourself, your family and your community. You must be extremely aware.

What's happening? Why is it happening? and what needs to be done? So you can make the best decisions and ensure everything can move smoothly to the best of your authority.

Because God will hold you accountable.

s.hukr

Mumin Mindset

Having knowledge of the Quran is such an advantage in life. People will try to argue and fight with me, concerning something about life and I will politely destroy them by referring to the speech of God.

Or I can use my knowledge to remove doubt from troubled hearts by referring to certain verses. This is why I would rather someone purchase a translated Quran than to purchase one of my books.

Allah's words have so much weight. You need to invest time into understanding your creator.

s.hukr

Mumin Mindset

Nearly all men can stand adversity but if you want to test a man's character, give him power. Then watch who conquers who?

s.hukr

Mumin Mindset

You know what's funny? Whenever I hear about a marriage and the girl is so happy saying things like "I married my best friend." or "I found my soulmate."

Funny because in about 6-12 months they are divorced and hate each other.

Lowkey sad, but HILARIOUS.

Absolute clown energy. They say the most outlandish things and publicise it. Keep your blessings private if you actually want to keep them.

s.hukr

Mumin Mindset

Fake Muslims, there are so many of them. People who say they are Muslim, but they are just lying to themselves and the whole world.

They are the hypocrites. Allah curses them in the Quran. They are the worst type of people. You need to avoid them.

There is no room for hypocrisy in Islam. You're either a Muslim or you aren't.

s.hukr

Mumin Mindset

Men can marry a woman for 4 reasons and the best is always deen. But women should always marry a man who has good deen and character.

Imagine a world where all women refused to marry a corrupt man or immediately had a divorce if they didn't take care of her properly.

Women are powerful if only they knew. Women have the ability to select the best leaders for the next generation and discard incompetent men and their lineage.

This is why education is so important for women. They need to recognise quickly the difference between good men and great men.

The difference between good women and great women, and then work towards becoming a great person.

s.hukr

Mumin Mindset

Men are logical, we either love with all our heart or we don't. We either go left or we go right. It's a straightforward decision. We see the world in a binary fashion.

But women don't do that. They are emotional. They could love you one day and hate you the next. They fluctuate like a cosine wave. They are like a quadratic equation that has both a positive and negative answer. They see the world through their feelings.

How wonderful it must be. And yet Allah made one compatible with the other. Another sign for a people who believe.

s.hukr

Mumin Mindset

1% of people actually want to change.

99% of people say they want to change but never do or take 20 years to change one thing about themselves.

s.hukr

Mumin Mindset

The truth is heavy, so do not make it heavier with your bad manners.

s.hukr

Mumin Mindset

Success always comes from Allah,
either to test you or to reward you.

s.hukr

Mumin Mindset

A man provides from his wealth. A woman does not. A woman doesn't need to make money to help her husband. She can if she wants too, but it is not her responsibility, it is not her burden to bear.

Rather a real woman would inspire the man to be greater. To become closer to Allah. And that would be a better way to increase his Rizq.

s.hukr

Mumin Mindset

Put people to shame by your sheer
will for what you believe is right.

Let your determination and success cause an
ignition of adrenaline for people to reach the
path of responsibility, utter respect and
undeniable truth.

s.hukr

Mumin Mindset

Write poetry and people will love you.
Write the truth and people will hate you.
That's the world I live in.

s.hukr

Mumin Mindset

Love her through your prayers, your poetry and your patience. Light up her heart with flowing rivers of eternal bliss.

Hold her hand and remind her of the beauty of Paradise. Accompany her through her moments of pain and her moments of joy. Be there for her whenever she needs you. Keep her happy and love her like she never felt love before.

And I swear she will never betray you; she will never undermine you, she will never take advantage of you. She will be your biggest blessing in this world and in the hereafter.

s.hukr

Mumin Mindset

Ordinary people give plenty of ordinary advice. But how can you surpass ordinary with it?

Not a millionaire? Don't discuss money.
Not an athlete? Don't discuss fitness.
Not a sheikh? Don't discuss knowledge.
You want extreme outliers.

People who are the top 1%. Their knowledge is beyond you. You run many times further in training than you do in the race. This is how you excel.

When you go to another dude, who is expert in his field for advice you need to learn 100% of what that guy knows to pull it off like him.

Extreme outliers are the only people to learn from. In any field. Beware, the advice of ordinary people.

s.hukr

Mumin Mindset

80% of arguments start because someone hasn't eaten. Brother, make sure you cook and feed your wife.

s.hukr

Mumin Mindset

Be humble.

Never think you are better than anyone else.
You are dust and onto dust you shall return.

s.hukr

Mumin Mindset

Small Circle.

Life Private.

Mind at Peace.

Destination Jannah.

s.hukr

Mumin Mindset

A healthy mind and heart come from a healthy diet. A strong mind and heart come from fasting often.

s.hukr

Mumin Mindset

You know you're living a good life
when you are happy to die tomorrow.

Who doesn't want to meet Allah?

s.hukr

Mumin Mindset

Womenkind were made
from the ribs of man.

You can't straighten it.
So don't bother.

Instead, be kind, gentle
and patient with them.

Don't allow disrespect
but also don't be so harsh.

s.hukr

Mumin Mindset

Chase this Dunya and it will ruin you.

Chase Allah with a passion and watch this world will start chasing you.

s.hukr

Mumin Mindset

An ingredient of success is a person who is always early or on time, but never late.

Time is the most valuable asset we all have. A finite amount of resource with an expiration date that nobody knows.

If you value your time, you will automatically value other people's time.

If you value my time, you will be rewarded. I like people who understand value.

It's about principle and respect.

s.hukr

Mumin Mindset

Don't assume something negative and if you do, cover it with the same love Allah covers your sins.

s.hukr

Mumin Mindset

When you give charity, don't even
let your hands know how much you give.

Be so generous and sincere that
Allah always doubles your investment.

s.hukr

Mumin Mindset

You are either with me until the end or you are against me. I absolutely hate people who sit on the fence trying to satisfy both sides.

You can't hold hands with your friends and your enemy at the same time. Pick a side.

And be honourable enough to meet the consequences if you lose.

s.hukr

Mumin Mindset

You know what's funny?

Every year. People spending their energy to see fancy lights in the night sky.

Fireworks. They call it.

People who follow other people.
They have no mind of their own.

s.hukr

Mumin Mindset

Sometimes I meet new people. They happen to notice my blessings and get all happy by it.

Then they want to become associated to me, so they become closer to my blessings and it may increase their status. Little do they know that every blessing that I have attained is an Amanah from Allah.

And I can't share the Amanah with anyone until Allah allows it. I have a duty to fulfill as do you. Focus on your duty and I know my lord is the most generous.

s.hukr

Mumin Mindset

The unity of this ummah begins from the unity of your family. All Muslims must be unified in core ideas, values, and beliefs.

But is your family unified? And if not what are you going to do about it?

s.hukr

Mumin Mindset

I do not want my peace disturbed at night by humans. I want to sleep and be woken up by angels for Thajjud. I want to talk to the most merciful, the most generous and the most powerful.

Do not disturb my peace at night. Tell me whatever you want during the day.

s.hukr

Mumin Mindset

Strong men can marry multiple women
and keep them all happy and satisfied.

But I live in a world surrounded
by weak men.

s.hukr

Mumin Mindset

Brother I suggest you start living alone. Away from family, away from all the distractions of life. Just focus on yourself. You'll start to realise and appreciate everything.

Don't focus on getting a good job or getting married. Or whatever your surroundings tell you. Listen to the darkness of the night.

Let your soul find foundations of what it means to be a man. Let Allah guide you and mould you into a soldier. Or else you may live a life without purpose and full of regret.

s.hukr

Mumin Mindset

You lose your own self respect when you become a slave of your desires and emotions.

s.hukr

Mumin Mindset

A strong man is not someone
with a lot of muscles or money.

A strong man is someone with a lot
of responsibility, respect and piety.

s.hukr

Mumin Mindset

If the journey of this Dunya was easy,
then how would life be a test?

s.hukr

Mumin Mindset

Positioning.

You must position yourself in a way that you can be valuable to yourself, and only then can you become valuable to others.

How can you help someone with money, if you are without an income, how can you help someone with advice if you don't read books. How can you help your wife, if you never did the dishes or know how to do the laundry.

You must constantly position yourself to learn the greatest number of skills and attain the greatest number of resources.

Position yourself in a way that will benefit you, not in a selfish way but in a way that serves the most value to others without expecting anything in return.

s.hukr

Mumin Mindset

Some men are so powerful and fearless that you get afraid at the thought of doing something wrong. God's warriors.

I like those men. They keep accountability. Fearless men with a simple goal of worshiping Allah alone without any partners.

Those are the men I admire.

s.hukr

Mumin Mindset

Most people have a negative mindset.

The way you think, the way you approach life, your behaviours, your attitudes, your way of thinking, your perspective of yourself and your reality. They shape the world you live in.

Is it positive or it is negative?

s.hukr

Mumin Mindset

People don't understand.

There is a billion dollars worth of value hidden inside of you, maybe more.

You are the most sophisticated creation of Allah. Doctors study 10+ years to understand a part of the human body and still they cannot cure every disease, they don't fully understand every mechanism of the human body.

There is no camera that comes close to the human eye, there is no computer that comes close to the intelligence of the human mind. Please understand, you are God's best creation, you need to believe in that. Believe in yourself.

Not out of pride but in humility and confidence that Allah created you in the best way and there is so much potential inside you.

Use this potential for the sake of Allah. Show the angels and the devils, why Allah declared you His best creation.

s.hukr

Mumin Mindset

Never marry an insecure woman
unless you are a very patient man.

Never marry an emotional man no
matter how patient of a woman you are.

s.hukr

Mumin Mindset

Taking a woman out of her masculine era and putting her in her feminine energy is a real man's job, not for silly boys.

s.hukr

Mumin Mindset

Never put your children above your wife. Allah first then your wife and then your children.

Your blood will so easily betray you if you betray the blessing from Allah.

s.hukr

Mumin Mindset

I am nobody.

I am a pile of
dust and bones.

But people keep
complimenting me.

What a gift from
God I have received.

s.hukr

Mumin Mindset

If you ever feel like you are having a bad day.
Look up. At the sky. And ponder a bit. Remind
yourself that someone is watching you.

Imagine how that someone will react
if you remain grateful despite it not
going as you would like. Imagine the
reward of patience & gratitude.

Most people don't deserve it.
But you aren't most people.

s.hukr

Mumin Mindset

When I look upon the majority of
Muslims today. I see them sleeping.

We have a book and a religion that is
quite literally a blueprint for excellence
and success in every aspect of life.
We should be the top 1% of society.

But we are addicted to our phones, our
self-comforting philosophies and ideas.
We happily convince ourselves that we
are good for doing the bare minimum.

We are sleeping and when someone
tries to wake us up, we get mad at them.
Fine, keep sleeping.

s.hukr

Mumin Mindset

Sins have many side-effects.

One of them is that they steal knowledge from you.

s.hukr

Mumin Mindset

Become such an attractive soul that women fall in love with you so easily.

s.hukr

Mumin Mindset

Don't chase this Dunya because you will never be able to. The art is to have this Dunya chase you and never let it catch up to you.

s.hukr

Mumin Mindset

Females are beautiful in every sense of the word. They can be covered head to toe, with only their eyes showing and still some guy will say, "O you have beautiful eyes." But I cannot relate, I don't find women beautiful like that.

I think the real beauty lies hidden beneath their eyes and around their soul. It is the favour of joy and delight you feel when you are in their presence. It's how she makes me feel that make me find her so attractive. Her outward appearance will fade in time, but the beauty of her soul will only increase in age.

Perhaps I am an old man that finds most females so boring.

s.hukr

Mumin Mindset

Some men go through so much and tell nobody their story. I know of men who sleep in their broken cars, have not eaten fresh food for many days and yet still get up and go to work.

I know of men who don't have a home, they don't have a fancy bed to sleep on. They don't have money to eat, they don't have a family to rely on. Heck, some left their families because of how toxic they are.

Some are disabled, they have chronic illnesses that effect their everyday living. They have lost their strength to do wonderful work. But still, you see them smiling and saying everything will be okay.

My heart bleeds for them because I know they cry in the secrecy of the nights, and they have no idea what they are doing with their lives. They just have hope in Allah.

They don't complain. They don't shout for attention. They don't beg or ask people for help. May Allah's mercy always be with those men.

s.hukr

Mumin Mindset

Imagine you have a friend who is on deen. They protect their awrah at all costs. Takes care of you in your time of need.

Doesn't let you do unislamic things because they don't want you going to hell. A friend that goes out of his way to make sure you smile. That would be nice. Be that friend for your friends.

s.hukr

Mumin Mindset

A great magnitude of power comes from giving without any expectations. To give so graciously that it makes people sense an awe of power.

s.hukr

Mumin Mindset

Show Allah your dedication towards the Quran and Sunnah and watch how your name becomes famous in the 7 heavens.

s.hukr

Mumin Mindset

I am nothing but a traveller on my journey to my grave. I hope to collect many good deeds and win as many hearts as possible.

Who are you and what are you doing?

s.hukr

Mumin Mindset

I stopped planning my life. I stopped trying to make everything fall into a perfect picture.

I stopped caring about things that don't matter. Things that cause me unnecessary stress, anxiety, and pain. Things I don't have control over. Letting go and having full Tawakul in Allah is so therapeutic.

All you need to do is focus on pleasing Allah and He will automatically take care of your life. He will open and close doors for you that you never even dreamed about.

s.hukr

Mumin Mindset

Maintain a deep understanding & connection with people who you engage with on a daily basis. Trust me, it will help you so much.

Understand their flaws, their weaknesses, their problems. Understand their potential, their strengths and their talents.

Understand their personality, their perspective, their habits, their story. Understand them such that you can see life in their shoes and use that to your advantage in a positive way.

If you can't do this with every person, at least do this with your spouse and your children.

s.hukr

Mumin Mindset

If your wife tells you to shave your beard.
Tell her you are going to get a second wife.

s.hukr

Mumin Mindset

A Dua from the heart:

O Allah If I have you it is as if I have everything in this world and if I don't have you, it is as if I have lost everything.

O Allah do not replace me, let me serve you to the best of my ability. Let me worship you as if I see you.

s.hukr

Mumin Mindset

To come home each night and be so deeply understood by you would be the great gift of my life.

s.hukr

Mumin Mindset

Understand that everything can be a blessing. It's just a matter of perspective. Be happy that you're broke, that you don't have many friends, that you don't have your dream job.

Be happy that you don't have everything that you desire. In that is a blessing that perhaps you'll see later in life.

s.hukr

Mumin Mindset

Being a man doesn't excuse you from your household duties. Go wash the dishes, clean your room and help around the house.

s.hukr

Mumin Mindset

Every time my wife wears too much makeup or wear something funny, all I'm going to say is, why do you look like a clown?

And bully her until she comes back dressed like a damn Queen, cos that's who I married, and she better know that.

s.hukr

Mumin Mindset

We may never speak again but know that you will forever remain in my conversations with Allah.

s.hukr

Mumin Mindset

Make millions but never let it show.

Love will all your heart
but never say "I love you".

Spread the aura of your soul
wherever you go, so that when
you meet death, there are
thousands of people who ensure
your safety to Paradise.

Live like a slave of God but
die as a king of hearts.

s.hukr

Mumin Mindset

Never idolise anyone
because that leads to shirk.

Admire them, show respect
and love but never become
head over heels for someone
that you think is an amazing person.

We all have flaws especially the
influencers that you look up to.

Also don't disrespect, dishonour and
insult people because you found out
their dirty secret. It is better that you
help them in a professional manner.

s.hukr

Mumin Mindset

It's difficult. It really is.

It's difficult seeing your loved ones not being able to understand you. It is difficult seeing them neglect their ability to become better people.

Sometimes letting go and creating distance is the best thing you can do.

s.hukr

Mumin Mindset

You know you are doing something right when people start sharing your work.

Some people call it stealing, I call it love.

s.hukr

Mumin Mindset

She has weak Eman when she doesn't believe in the idea of polygyny.

s.hukr

Mumin Mindset

Just like diamonds that are hidden beneath layers of rock and dirt.

It is the same with righteous souls that are hidden away from everyone.

s.hukr

Mumin Mindset

People don't understand how
health is such a Nimah.

Especially while you are
young and full of energy.

Maybe you'll appreciate it
more as time passes.

s.hukr

Mumin Mindset

Wealth is nothing more than a tool of responsibility that men should use in the best interest of society, in the best interest of the Divine order.

Unfortunately, many people allow wealth to control them. You can easily see this happen to people who show off their material possessions for fame, status and to please their uncontrollable desires.

s.hukr

Mumin Mindset

A few words and you can
make someone's blood boil.

A few words and you can
steal someone's heart.

A few words and you can
manipulate their beliefs.

It only takes a few words to
control most people.

s.hukr

Mumin Mindset

Introverts aren't anti-social, they just hate drama, stupidity and fake people.

s.hukr

Mumin Mindset

Young men love to be successful, but
I barely see them come to the place of
success, the place for your 5 daily prayers.

s.hukr

Mumin Mindset

Your mind is a weapon, keep it loaded.

Don't play small, play ambitious.

s.hukr

Mumin Mindset

Every time you open your mouth.
You reveal something about yourself.

Better to remain a silent mystery.

s.hukr

Mumin Mindset

Very few women are worthy of receiving the depth of a man's love.

s.hukr

Mumin Mindset

It's easy for me to show off my wealth, status and beauty to impress people, but I don't.

I don't want temporary things to define me and neither should you.

Keep decorating the soul.

s.hukr

Mumin Mindset

Be there for people when they need you,
when they are at their lowest.

And stay away when they want you,
when they are in their good times.

That's the type of man I am.

s.hukr

Mumin Mindset

People tell me they have no time.
Which I find to be a lie.

Get a **Nokia 3310**.

Then watch how much
free time you have.

s.hukr

Mumin Mindset

If you want a happy life, live simply.
There is so much peace in it.

s.hukr

Mumin Mindset

A man with outstanding character
is he who says the right words
at the right time.

Sometimes that means not
saying anything.

s.hukr

Mumin Mindset

I don't care if the world is burning. I don't care how many lives are lost. That's a small issue in the grand scheme of things.

I want the diseases in the hearts of Muslims to disappear. I want to see Muslims loving one another like they used too. I want to see unity and bounds that would last eternity.

I would like to see Muslims become the inheritors of this world. Because right now we are not worthy of such authority.

We have become defiantly disobedient.

s.hukr

Mumin Mindset

When I meet new people, I don't like telling them who I am and what I've done.

Because I don't like being
given special treatment.

I rather they treat me
as a fellow stranger.

s.hukr

Mumin Mindset

My beauty or lack of comes from my soul, not my heritage or place of birth.

My destination of origin adds no value to me instead creates borders of separation within your mind that you follow so damn religiously.

Don't ask me where I'm from cos I will reply with my "my mother's belly".

s.hukr

Mumin Mindset

Before you even attempt to understand this world. Start by understanding yourself.

Understand yourself through the eyes of the devil and never let him exploit you.

He is your clear enemy.

s.hukr

Mumin Mindset

People will betray you,
they will hurt you,
they will make you cry
and make you feel so insignificant.

Sometimes it's your own family or
the people you care about the most.

Don't become hopeless,
don't become sad.
Don't let this world make
you sour and full of hate.

Use this hidden blessing as a
way to become closer to Allah.

He understands you more
than anyone. Rely on Allah.
Trust Allah. With Sabr,
things will get better.

I promise you.

s.hukr

Mumin Mindset

God gives his greatest battles
to his strongest soldiers.

A servant of God can adapt
to any human endeavour.

"Be and it is."

s.hukr

Mumin Mindset

I know I make generalisations.

But that's the point. It's quite an effective way to prove a point about the masses. I don't have time to pinpoint every outlier, every exceptional situation. Nor do you have time to get upset over trivial things.

Exceptions do not disprove generalisations. Intelligent people use generalisations because it's a convenient way to get you to understand a certain point of view. Stop being so sensitive.

s.hukr

Mumin Mindset

I don't understand why people dislike fruits
and vegetables. They have so many benefits.

If you want good skin and a healthy body,
control what you eat. Especially the females
who put layers of makeup.

Correct the root of the issue,
don't just mask it.

s.hukr

Mumin Mindset

Weak men follow the instructions of women and other men.

Strong men follow the instructions of Allah.

s.hukr

Mumin Mindset

The ideas and perspectives I try to share are there to wake you up from your delusional day to day life and make you ponder of a world outside your own reality.

s.hukr

Mumin Mindset

The person I needed the most in life never came. God made me realise that all you need is Him. He is the king of Kings.

s.hukr

Mumin Mindset

Solitude with God is a kind of price you have to pay for a certain complexity of mind.

s.hukr

Mumin Mindset

Let the sheep's of this world sleep.
Let them waste their life on futile nonsense.

For you are on a path of great abundance,
a path to the seven heavens.

A journey of **Ihsan**.

s.hukr

Mumin Mindset

I dislike men who follow everything their mother or wife says. Is she the man of the house, or are you?

s.hukr

Mumin Mindset

While everyone else is sleeping,
it is the perfect opportunity to
get things done.

Less people. Less problems.
Less interruptions.
More efficiency.

More clarity. More peace.
And more power to you.

Starting your day with Fajr is
your biggest advantage in life.

s.hukr

Mumin Mindset

If she is pretty, don't compliment her looks.

Be mean, be a little sour and salty.
Be memorable and different.
Show a bit of your heart.
But always remain respectful.

She isn't going to remember you if you
are just like every other guy she has met.

Bring out the best in her by not complimenting
her. Be a little savage. Show her that her
beauty isn't what you value in her.

s.hukr

Mumin Mindset

Calm masculine men with **Haya**.

That's her weakness.

s.hukr

Mumin Mindset

Make real connections with people who add a lot of value into your life without asking for anything in return.

s.hukr

Mumin Mindset

Be Decisive in life.

Take action even if your decision is wrong. Taking action and falling down is better than taking no action and not learning from your fall.

Life is meant to be an adventure where you choose your paths, you make certain decisions that lead you to certain places.

If you get lost, that's part of the journey, it's part of the fun. Overtime you will get better at making decisions. But you should never be indecisive because you are afraid or ignorant.

Be willing to take risk in your life.
No risk. No reward.

s.hukr

Mumin Mindset

Being alone is easy when you
enjoy your own company.

Most people don't like being alone,
they don't like who they are.

Their soul knows it too well.

s.hukr

Mumin Mindset

Some men rely on external confidence like a fast car, big muscles or public display of wealth.

Women do the same with makeup, outfits and what not.

I call it fake confidence
for fake people.

s.hukr

Mumin Mindset

I actually hate culture.

In some cultures, it's rude to come early. In some cultures, it's okay to open a door without knocking. In some cultures, people have to fight to pay the dinner bill. In some cultures, yelling is normal and being quiet is seen as being shy.

In some cultures, men can't cook or clean, they just work and make money. In some cultures, husband and wife do 50 / 50. In some cultures, haram is normalised, and halal is considered as extreme religious behaviour.

But I love Islam.

It's such a peaceful and balanced way of living. It is according to Allah's instructions, what He has ordained for us. It is very beautiful, simple, and easy. That's what I strive for.

But unfortunately, more than half the Muslim population follows culture not Islam.

s.hukr

Mumin Mindset

The reason a lot of youngsters are falling into Haram is because the generation before failed to make Halal easy. Don't repeat the same mistakes.

s.hukr

Mumin Mindset

Women don't care about your height, your
status, your wealth, your job or whatever
she is going to ask you about.

It's a social mechanism they use
to see your character, to see how
you speak, your energy, your vibe,
how you carry yourself. The things
you respect and value.

That's what they care about.

They want to see how you make them
feel, it's all about the feelings for them.

They are emotional beings and
there's nothing wrong with that.

s.hukr

Mumin Mindset

Men are direct and straight forward; we get to the point in a logical manner. But women are indirect, they go around the bush and are sensitive when things are straight forward.

You must understand the nature of women and use this knowledge to become a better provider, a better husband, a better brother and a better man. Too often I have seen men act like women. I find that so revolting.

s.hukr

Mumin Mindset

When your focus is Allah,
every action becomes worship,
to the one worthy of all worship.

s.hukr

Mumin Mindset

May the angel of death arrive when you
and I become the most righteous.

May he come during the
month of Ramadan.

s.hukr

Mumin Mindset

Be kind. Be open minded.

Be a seeker of knowledge.

Be full of love, full of compassion.

Be surrounded by likeminded individuals.

These things are important.

These things will help you attain Jannah.

s.hukr

Mumin Mindset

Just imagine you're reading a book or watching a drama series where the main character only changes for one month and then continues his mediocre life, boring right?

Now look at yourself after Ramadan.

s.hukr

Mumin Mindset

Never let her pay for food,
clothing or anything essential.

"Men are the caretakers of women."

s.hukr

Mumin Mindset

I live in a world where common sense has become glorified.

O Allah for how much longer do I have to stay in this prison?

s.hukr

Mumin Mindset

I avoid women.
Women avoid you.

We are not the same.

s.hukr

Mumin Mindset

One day when I become wealthy.

I will buy every church in my town
and turn it into a mosque.

I will buy every restaurant
and make it halal.

I will buy every clothing
shop and turn it modest.

I will make halal easy and abundant,
and haram difficult and scarce.

As long as Allah allows it.
It will happen.

s.hukr

Mumin Mindset

Be early to success.

Be early to your Salah.

Never delay a meeting with Allah.

You need Him.

He doesn't need you.

Always make a good impression.

s.hukr

Mumin Mindset

Being rich isn't bad.
Greed is.

Being religious isn't bad.
Arrogance is.

Being smart isn't bad.
Selfishness is.

Being powerful isn't bad.
Ignorance is.

s.hukr

Mumin Mindset

Everyone believes in something. Even the non-
believers. They believe in the idea of not believing.
And your beliefs shape your world.

It's up to you to consistently hold your
beliefs accountable towards the truth.

Do your beliefs match the
Quran and Sunnah?
or do they go against it?

For if your beliefs are upon
the truth you will remain
victorious otherwise your
beliefs will be jeopardising
your own success.

And don't tell me you believe
in something but you actually don't.
That is the definition of a hypocrite.

s.hukr

Mumin Mindset

Forgive people even if they
don't deserve it.

Your heart should be full
of mercy not for them,
but to impress Allah.

If you expect Allah to have
mercy on you, you must
have mercy on His people.

s.hukr

Mumin Mindset

How to Test a Muslim Girl.

1. Tell her you don't like her culture, or her outfit then just watch her reaction.

2. Ask about her definition of Haya and Hijab. Pay close attention to what she says and how she says it.

3. Ignore her for an extended amount of time and watch the clock.

s.hukr

Mumin Mindset

Women don't like nice men.

They like dangerous mean fearless men who are capable of being respectful and honest.

s.hukr

Mumin Mindset

Stop chasing this Dunya.

The art is to have this Dunya chase you and never let it catch up to you.

s.hukr

Mumin Mindset

You must maintain clarity, so you can maintain order and so you can achieve greatness.

s.hukr

Mumin Mindset

People are afraid of things they don't
understand. Afraid of the unknown.

They are afraid to stand their ground.
Afraid of losing, afraid of taking risk.

Afraid of rejection.
Afraid of what others think.

Keep your fears far away from me.
For a real man only fears Allah.

s.hukr

Mumin Mindset

I avoid women.
I avoid a quick and easy life.
I avoid things that make me weak.

I've noticed the further away I stay away from pleasure and comfort, the stronger I become.
I like being strong.

s.hukr

Mumin Mindset

The person I am today is a different person to the one 5 years ago. The person 5 years in the future will be different to the person I am today. I must continuously change, improve, and adapt to my situations.

Because Allah doesn't change your condition to something better if you aren't willing to change yourself into someone better.

s.hukr

Mumin Mindset

What comes naturally to me took
me many years of experience,
comprehension and hard work.

I never stopped learning.
I am constantly learning from
people, places, things and experiences.

The moment you stop learning
from everything and everyone.

Is the moment you have decided
to neglect God's instruction and
thus decided to destroy your future.

s.hukr

Mumin Mindset

The poor hate the rich.
The fat hate the fit.
The ignorant hates the intelligent.
The weak hate the strong.

Why? Because hating is easy.
Love isn't.

s.hukr

Mumin Mindset

Wealth. Status and Beauty.

This isn't success for a Muslim.

It's just a side effect. A side quest.

A biproduct of worshipping
Allah without any partners.

s.hukr

Mumin Mindset

Weak men will allow injustice, lies and corruption to take place in their presence.

A strong man will confront the idiot who thought it was a good idea.

I will not allow bad things to happen to good people in my presence and neither should you.

s.hukr

Mumin Mindset

Start your day with Bismillah
and end it with Ayatul Kursi.

Wakeup early and sleep early.
You'll be in the express
lane for Jannah too.

s.hukr

Mumin Mindset

I've come to notice that most people
don't like me because I speak the truth.

They want me to tell lies that they
are so used to hearing.

Sorry but I hate lies.

s.hukr

Mumin Mindset

There is something that you desire, that you plan for, that you work towards. And there is something that Allah desires for you and plans for you.

If you go after what you desire, God will make you tired and it won't happen as you want until you realise you have to go after what Allah wants from you.

If you run towards Allah, serve Him, do what He wants you to do, you will also get what you desire.

How can Allah not give you what you want, while you serve Him in the best of manners?

s.hukr

Mumin Mindset

Remember, they are going to misunderstand you, perhaps even hate you. Not because you are a bad person. But because you are better.

There is a price for wisdom, success, honour and piety. Most people will never know.

s.hukr

Mumin Mindset

What good is money if my
ummah is still suffering?

What good is first class
if my family can't sit?

What good is being intelligent
when people won't take any benefit?

I can't seem to interfere with Allah's
plan no matter how much it pains me.

It's so lonely at the top.
No matter how much I try.
I can't control the destiny of others.

Their fate is in their hands.
All I can do is pray for them
and trust Allah to do what is best.

s.hukr

Mumin Mindset

People don't need to know who you are and what you have done.

God will raise your honour and respect automatically according to His Divine Principles.

s.hukr

Mumin Mindset

Learn about the Pareto principle. Something they will not teach you at school.

It is how you will apply leverage in a way that will benefit your entire life.

s.hukr

Mumin Mindset

Understand the bell curve distribution.
Then apply it to the real world.

It will give you a competitive edge.

s.hukr

Mumin Mindset

Always strive for exponential growth.

It is by far the most difficult to achieve but worth every sweat, blood and tear.

Initially the growth is less than linear but over time it compounds and that's what you need to aim for.

s.hukr

Mumin Mindset

Men are not judged by their words.
They are judged by their actions.

Act more. Say nothing.

s.hukr

Mumin Mindset

You become a dangerous man when you can make women fall in love with you without even trying. The rare breed of man never chase, they attract.

s.hukr

Mumin Mindset

Don't fear me, I am nothing
but a man of God's principles.

The principles however
you should fear.

They have destroyed many
generations before you.

s.hukr

Mumin Mindset

Once you reach a certain level of status, wealth and ultimately power. People will become afraid of you.

They will fear your justice because it doesn't benefit them. They will fear your truth because it doesn't suit their whims and desires.

And they will fear you because you are a man of Allah. That's the type of man you need to become.

s.hukr

Mumin Mindset

Women love love.

They love the idea of falling in love.
They love having their emotions
fuelled by someone who they adore.

They love a man who can be emotional
with them, care for them. Be sweet, kind
and compassionate. They love surprises,
meaningful conversations and gifts.

Never be unkind to a woman even if
she is being unreasonable. A woman's
dua is like a gift from the heavens.

Collect as many as you can.

s.hukr

Mumin Mindset

If my wife expects me to celebrate her birthday. She isn't my wife.

I don't celebrate my own birthday, what makes you think I'll celebrate yours?

I am a Muslim, not a munafiq.

s.hukr

Mumin Mindset

When you see a person who is often silent and avoids people. Yet successful in his Deen and Dunya.

Try to stay close to him. Because he has been given wisdom from Allah.

s.hukr

Mumin Mindset

Lazy people will drag themselves down in life and drag others with them.

They are like black holes.
Stay away from lazy people.

Stay away from people who complain and blame others for their own inability to make things better.

s.hukr

Mumin Mindset

As long as your mindset does
not defer from Allah's book,
you are destined for success.

But most people do not
follow His book.

s.hukr

Mumin Mindset

You need to become the man that has an alliance with God. Who is admired by his family and feared by his foes.

s.hukr

Mumin Mindset

I know people are annoying.
I know people can be difficult.
I know people can be stupid,
stubborn and selfish.

I know that people have flaws
and you may not always see good
in them. But believe that there is
an atoms weight of good in them.

Your reward is with Allah.

s.hukr

Mumin Mindset

Some souls will not find comfort in this world. They will not find belonging. They will find it hard to fit in because of how different they are.

That is their fate. They will drift from one journey to another with a compass that always points back to God.

They will continue to suppress their desire for things this world could never deliver. What a treasured soul they must be?

s.hukr

Mumin Mindset

Most people live in a house not a home.

A home to me is a place of security, peace, and love. There should be order at home, not chaos. There should be boundaries and rules. There should be enough comfort to rejuvenate. Facilities of care and rest. There should be a sense of safety and peace of mind. Thats the bare minimum of what home should be.

s.hukr

Mumin Mindset

When you have Allah,
you have everything.

When you don't,
you have nothing.

s.hukr

Mumin Mindset

Humble enough to know
I can lose everything.

Confident enough to know
I can get it all back.

s.hukr

Mumin Mindset

I love people in silence.
I love them in their time of need.
I love them when nobody loves them.

This is a fragment of the love
Allah has for you. But do you love
Allah like the ocean loves the moon?

s.hukr

Mumin Mindset

The way Allah covers my sins with a veil,
is the same way I cover the sins of people
in front of other people.

I can be a dangerous enemy but my heart
would rather choose mercy and forgiveness.

s.hukr

Mumin Mindset

O Men, wakeup.

Become God's fearless warriors that you were designed to become. For how long will you stay asleep, living your insignificant life?

Hit the gym. Read more books. Protect your women. Study the life of the Prophet ﷺ.

Carry out righteous work in the name of Allah and then expect success.

s.hukr

Mumin Mindset

How can you sleep in peace knowing
your ummah is suffering injustice?

Do you not have a sense of duty
nor responsibility? How selfish
have you become?

s.hukr

Mumin Mindset

Comfort is when you look into
her eyes all you see is home.

Love is when she smiles at you
and takes away all your worries.

Happiness is when you hold
her hand and take her to Paradise.

s.hukr

Mumin Mindset

Men of power behave very differently.

We will remain unfazed even
if their whole world is burning.

We will have full Tawakul in Allah.

s.hukr

Mumin Mindset

Being a man is no easy task.

We go through so much adversity, so much pain and trauma. We turn off our feelings and do what is required. So we can provide for our loved ones. Be a source of happiness and comfort for others.

Even if those loved ones don't appreciate or love us back. Never think that men have it easier. We go through so much that we don't tell anyone. It's just between Allah.

s.hukr

Mumin Mindset

Is hijab a choice?
Is it a journey?
Is it a command from Allah?

I think you already know the answer.

s.hukr

Mumin Mindset

Most people:

- Lack discipline
- Lack patience
- Lack purpose
- Don't read
- Don't exercise
- Don't invest time

But you aren't most people,
you are a Muslim man.

Show people what that means.

s.hukr

Mumin Mindset

This Dunya owes you nothing.
Stop having expectations.

s.hukr

Mumin Mindset

Don't believe everything you hear.
Always do you due diligence.

s.hukr

Mumin Mindset

Your success is determined by your way of life and true Islamic monotheism encourages success in Dunya and in the afterlife.

The definition of success is not according to what you want or what I want or what people want from you. It is according to what Allah wants from you. He is our lord and we need to make Him our focus.

s.hukr

Mumin Mindset

The older you get, the more you just want someone with Iman in their heart, a warm smile and arms that hold you tight forever.

When you look at them, you are reminded of how lucky you are to be with them.

May you become a person who becomes worthy of this blessing. **Say Ameen.**

s.hukr

Mumin Mindset

My brother,

I highly suggest you start something extraordinary, where you can collect a house without Riba every year.

You need an income that can easily beat the inflation rate. You are the provider, and you need to fulfil your duty to the best of your ability.

Struggling with a 9 to 5 and then making your wife work will not cut it. Being ignorant and following everyone else will not cut it.

You need to dream bigger. You need a high-income skill. You need to be uncomfortable and build something that will affect hundreds and thousands of people.

s.hukr

Mumin Mindset

I don't understand you young people.

Allah has blessed with you with youth, strength in your bones and a functioning mind that is ready to perform. Why do you waste your time complaining?

Why are you ungrateful? With that kind of attitude, God will give you more to complain about. Stop wasting your time on meaningless things.

Get up early every morning, start praying fajr, start understanding the Quran. Invest in books, invest in yourself while you still have the ability.

Go get a job, find a side hustle, do something productive, something that adds value into yourself and in the lives of others. Get to a point where you can educate yourself on how to fix yourself and your environment.

There is knowledge out there to fix every problem similar to how there is a cure for every disease… but YOU have to go and find it. Get off your lazy bum and go find what you're looking for and at every intersection ask for God's guidance.

s.hukr

Mumin Mindset

Let me tell you something.

As men you must learn how to handle the women in your family with fairness and respect. Never allow your love for your wife to hinder the respect of your mother or sister. Neither allow your mother to hurt your relationship with your wife.

I see so many weak men fall victim to their love for women. Pathetic.

How can you win wars in the battlefield, if you can't win the battles within your own family that you have authority over?

s.hukr

Mumin Mindset

In an era of good looks, I still prefer personality, intelligence and God consciousness.

s.hukr

Mumin Mindset

Thank you for reading this book.

I hope that you enjoyed it and found some benefit from my words.

May Allah always have mercy on you and guide you towards the straight path. **Ameen.**

Sincerely,
s.hukr

Did you benefit from this book?
Then go get my other books.
Let's elevate together.

fajrnoor.com

S.hukr Books

1. Fajr and Noor

2. Through His Eyes

3. Noor upon Noor

4. Slice of Paradise

5. Mumin Mindset

6. How to Marry a Muslim Girl

7. Divine Love

www.ingramcontent.com/pod-product-compliance
Lightning Source LLC
Chambersburg PA
CBHW030255010526
44107CB00053B/1721